# BLUES HARP

## FROM SCRATCH

This book © Copyright 1998 by Wise Publications.

Book design by Niche.
Cover design by Michael Bell Design.
Edited by Pat Conway.
Music processed by Seton Music Graphics.
Printed in the UK.
Photographs courtesy of Redferns and London Features International.

All solos: Music by Mick Kinsella
© Copyright 1997 Campbell Connelly & Company Limited, 14-15 Berners Street, London W1.
All Rights Reserved, International Copyright Secured.
Except 'Oh Susanna' (page 8) and Amazing Grace (page 10):
Traditional.
Copyright 1997 Dorsey Brothers Music Limited, 14-15 Berners Street, London W1
All Rights Reserved. International Copyright Secured.

ISBN: 978-0-7119-4706-1

Visit Hal Leonard Online at
**www.halleonard.com**

Contact us:
**Hal Leonard**
7777 West Bluemound Road
Milwaukee, WI 53213
Email: info@halleonard.com

In Europe, contact:
**Hal Leonard Europe Limited**
42 Wigmore Street
Marylebone, London, W1U 2RY
Email: info@halleonardeurope.com

In Australia, contact:
**Hal Leonard Australia Pty. Ltd.**
4 Lentara Court
Cheltenham, Victoria, 3192 Australia
Email: info@halleonard.com.au

**Audio Track Listing**

1. Intro / The 'C' Scale - Exercise 1
2. C Scale - Exercises 2-7
3. Oh Susanna (solo)
4. The High Octave - Exercises 9 & 10
5. Amazing Grace (solo)
6. Blues Type Scale In G - Exercise 12
7. G Blues Scale - Exercises 13-16
8. Easy Street (solo)
9. Trouble Free Blues (solo)
10. D To D♭ Bend - Exercises 19 & 20
11. Sundrive Blues (solo)
12. A To A♭ Bend - Exercises 22-24
13. Note Bending Riffs - Exercises 25-28
14. Blue Mood (solo)
15. Hot Summer Blues (solo)
16. B To B♭ Bend - Exercises 31-33
17. Cloudy Skies (solo)
18. G To G♭ Bend - Exercises 35-37
19. Blues Riffs With Bends - Exercises 38-41
20. Downtown Blues (solo)
21. Three Is A Crowd (solo)
22. Full Tone Bends - Exercises 44-46
23. Full Tone Bend Riffs 47-50
24. Two Step Blues (solo)
25. Direct Bending - Exercises 52-55
26. Direct Bend Blues Riffs - Exercises 56-60
27. Blues Scale In G - Exercises 61 & 62
28. Blues Scale Riffs - Exercises 63-66
29. After Midnight (solo)
30. Blues Riffs - Exercises 68-76
31. Blow Bending - Exercise 77
32. Blow Bend Riffs - Exercises 78-82
33. High Time Blues (solo)
34. The Wah Wah - Exercises 84-86
35. Blues Riffs With "Wah Wah" - Exercises 87-90
36 Raining Down (solo)
37. The Head Roll - Exercises 92-94
38. Head Roll Riffs - Exercises 95-99
39. Rolling South (solo)
40. The Tongue Roll - Exercises 101-103
41. Tongue Roll Riffs - Exercises 104-108
42. Southern Jive (solo)
43. Tongue Roll & Wah Wah - Exercises 110 & 111
44. Blues Riffs With Tongue Roll And Wah Wah - Exercises 112-116
45. Trouble 'n' Booze (solo)
46. Shaking The Harp - Exercises 118 & 119
47. Throat & Jaw Vibrato - Exercises 120 & 121
48. Blues Riffs Using Tone Control - Exercises 122-125
49. Note Splitting - Exercises 126 & 127
50. Note Splitting Riffs - Exercises 128-132
51. Lake Shore Drive (solo)

How To Hold
The Harmonica
4

Signs And Symbols Used
In This Book
5

Notes On The Harmonica
5

Play A Scale
5

The 'C' Scale
5

C Scale Exercises
6

Playing In Triplets
6

Playing Staggered Notes
6

Straight Playing
7

Oh Sussana (solo)
8

The High Octave
9

Amazing Grace (solo)
10

Cross Playing
11

Cross Harp Positions
11

Blues Type Scale In G
11

G Blues Scale Exercises
12

Easy Street (solo)
13

Trouble Free Blues (solo)
14

Note Bending
16

D To D♭ Bend
16

Sundrive Blues (solo)
17

A To A♭ Bend
18

Note Bending Riffs:
D To D♭ and A To A♭ Bend
19

Blue Mood (solo)
20

Hot Summer Blues (solo)
21

B To B♭ Bend
23

Cloudy Skies (solo)
24

G To G♭ Bend
25

Blues Riffs With Bends
26

Downtown Blues (solo)
27

Three Is A Crowd (solo)
28

Full Tone Bends
30

Full Tone Bend Riffs
31

Two Step Blues (solo)
32

Direct Bending
33

Direct Bend Exercises
34

Direct Bend Blues Riffs
35

Blues Scale In G
36

Blues Scale Riffs
37

After Midnight (solo)
38

Blues Riffs
39

Blow Bending
41

Blow Bend Riffs
42

High Time Blues (solo)
43

The Wah Wah
44

Blues Riffs With "Wah Wah"
45

Raining Down (solo)
46

The Head Roll
47

Head Roll Riffs
48

Rolling South (solo)
49

The Tongue Roll
50

Tongue Roll Riffs
51

Southern Jive (solo)
52

Tongue Roll & Wah Wah
53

Blues Riffs With
Tongue Roll And Wah Wah
54

Trouble 'n' Booze (solo)
55

Vibrato
56

Throat Vibrato
57

Jaw Vibrato
57

Blues Riffs Using Tone Control
58

Note Splitting
59

Note Splitting Riffs
60

Lake Shore Drive (solo)
61

# HOW TO HOLD THE HARMONICA

You will notice that your harmonica has the numbers 1–10 on one side. Hold the instrument in your left hand with the number one, which is the lowest note, to the left. Place your right hand in the position shown below.

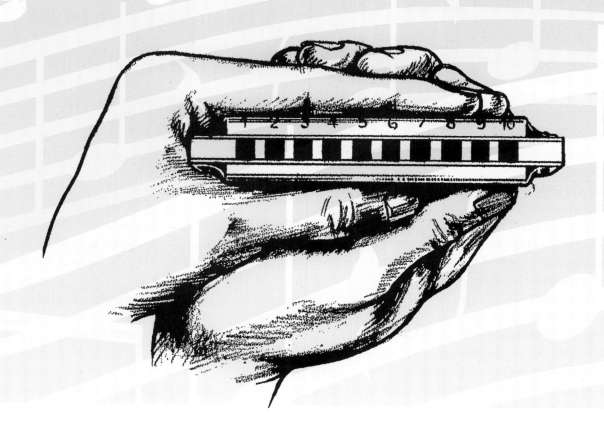

# THE PUCKER METHOD

Using the "Pucker" method you can play a single note cleanly and simply. The "Pucker" method is very similar to whistling. You pucker your lips, whistle a note, then move your mouth towards the harmonica, singling out the note you want to play. When you get the hang of it you should be able to play from one hole to another, clearly and without much trouble. When playing single notes on the harmonica, you should relax your lips but keep the pucker shape at all times.
Don't let any other note sound except the one that you are playing.
For good tone keep your mouth well sealed on the harmonica.

# SIGNS AND SYMBOLS USED IN THIS BOOK

↑   Indicates a blow note (exhale).
↓   Indicates a draw note (inhale).
③   A half circle underneath the music indicates a semitone (half step) bend.
③   A full circle underneath the music indicates a full tone (full step) bend.

# NOTES ON THE HARMONICA

# PLAY A SCALE

The first thing we learn to play on the harmonica is the C scale.
Try to play each note clearly, without interference from neighbouring notes.
This may be tedious at first, but with a little practice you will soon be able to
play each individual note.

# THE 'C' SCALE

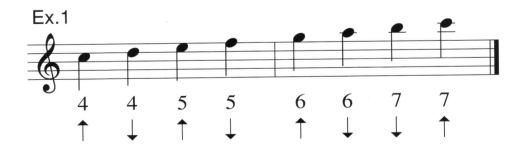

# C SCALE EXERCISES

Here are some exercises to help you to become familiar with the notes on the instrument. These exercises will help you to move easily from hole to hole while playing single notes and will also help you with your breathing.

In this descending exercise the C note on the 4th hole acts as a "pivot note". This is a great exercise for practising skipping holes.

Ex. 2

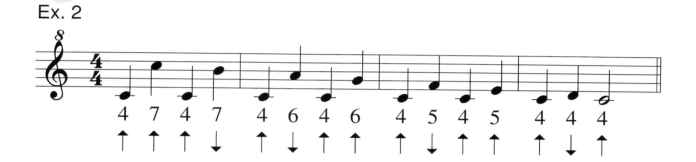

# PLAYING IN TRIPLETS

You shouldn't have any trouble with this exercise as the notes are adjacent to each other. The triplets are counted as: 1 and a, 2 and a, 3 and a.

Ex.3

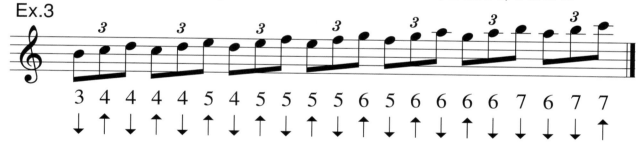

# PLAYING STAGGERED NOTES

This exercise features two draw notes and two blow notes in succession.

Ex.4

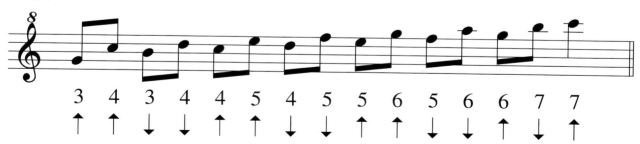

This time we play an ascending exercise with the C note as the "pivot note". Not only are these exercises great for learning to jump holes but they will also help you with your breathing as the breath direction keeps changing.

Ex.5

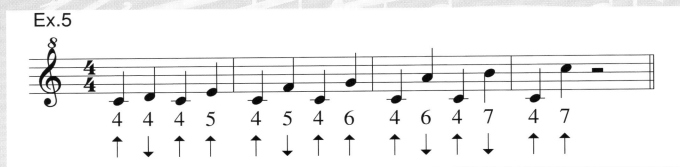

Now we will use the G on the 2nd hole as our "pivot note" in this descending exercise. Here's the last of our C scale exercises.

Ex.6

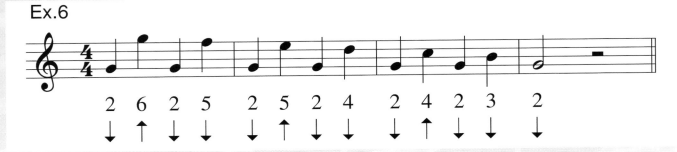

This time we ascend using the G as the "pivot note".

Ex.7

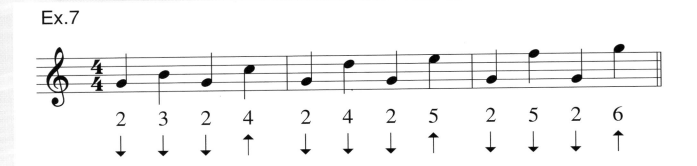

# STRAIGHT PLAYING

This type of playing is called 'Straight Playing' because the tunes are played in the natural key of the harmonica.
For example, with the C harmonica we will play in the key of C.

Although this is a blues book which features mainly note bending, we have included three straight tunes. This is to allow you to become familiar with the notes on the harmonica. All of the exercises and solos in this book will be played on the C harmonica.

# OH SUSANNA

Here is a well known tune which is played straight in the key of C.
It features holes 4, 5, and 6.
Play it slowly at first and increase the speed as you progress.
Remember, it is more important to play with accuracy than with speed ...
speed will come with practice.

# THE HIGH OCTAVE

From hole 7 to hole 10, a straight C scale can be played.
The B note which is produced by blow bending on hole 10 is very difficult to
play at this stage, so we will leave it out for the moment and just deal with the
incomplete scale of C.
When the sign *8* appears over the treble clef it indicates that the
music is played an octave higher than written.

Ex.9

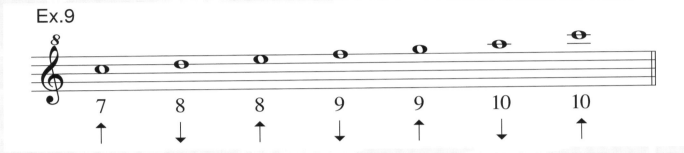

This time try playing both ascending and descending.

Ex.10

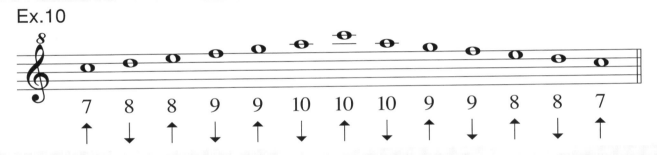

Junior Wells

9

# AMAZING GRACE

Here's another tune which is quite easy to play.
It's played on the top end of the harmonica using holes 6, 7, 8 and 9.

# CROSS PLAYING

Playing the harmonica in the "Cross Position" is essential for playing blues or country music etc., as it allows you to play with more expression and feeling.

"Cross Playing" also enables you to play in many keys and we will now deal with the key of G on our C harmonica. Your starting point will be a draw note on the 2nd hole which is G. In this position or key you will notice that there are more draw notes than blow notes used.

# CROSS HARP POSITIONS

| Key of Harp | A | B | C | D | E | F | G |
| --- | --- | --- | --- | --- | --- | --- | --- |
| Cross Key you will play in | E | F♯ | G | A | B | C | D |

# BLUES TYPE SCALE IN G

This scale will give you the feel of the 'Cross Playing' sound.
First play it ascending only and then both ascending and descending.

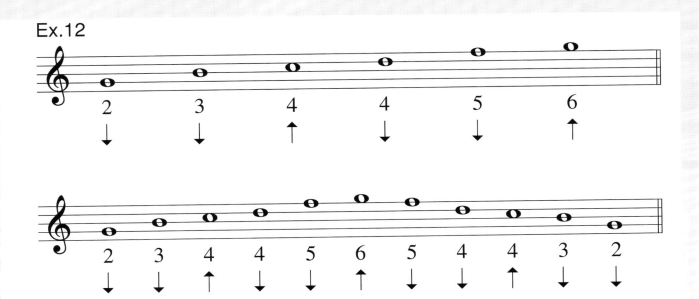

Ex.12

11

# G BLUES SCALE EXERCISES

Here are some exercises for you to practice on the G Blues Scale.
You should find them quite easy to play.

Ex.13

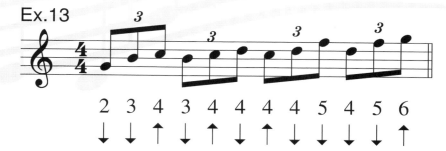

| 2 | 3 | 4 | 3 | 4 | 4 | 4 | 4 | 5 | 4 | 5 | 6 |
|---|---|---|---|---|---|---|---|---|---|---|---|
| ↓ | ↓ | ↑ | ↓ | ↑ | ↓ | ↑ | ↓ | ↓ | ↓ | ↓ | ↑ |

Ascending and descending triplet exercise.

Ex.14

| 2 | 3 | 4 | 3 | 4 | 4 | 4 | 4 | 5 | 4 | 5 | 6 |
|---|---|---|---|---|---|---|---|---|---|---|---|
| ↓ | ↓ | ↑ | ↓ | ↑ | ↓ | ↑ | ↓ | ↓ | ↓ | ↓ | ↑ |

| 5 | 4 | 5 | 4 | 4 | 4 | 4 | 3 | 4 | 3 | 2 | 2 |
|---|---|---|---|---|---|---|---|---|---|---|---|
| ↓ | ↓ | ↓ | ↓ | ↑ | ↓ | ↑ | ↓ | ↑ | ↓ | ↓ | ↓ |

Let's practice skipping holes for this next triplet exercise.

Ex.15

| 2 | 3 | 4 | 3 | 2 | 4 | 4 | 3 | 5 | 4 | 4 | 6 | 5 | 4 | 4 | 3 | 2 | 2 |
|---|---|---|---|---|---|---|---|---|---|---|---|---|---|---|---|---|---|
| ↓ | ↓ | ↑ | ↓ | ↓ | ↓ | ↓ | ↑ | ↓ | ↓ | ↓ | ↑ | ↑ | ↓ | ↓ | ↑ | ↓ | ↓ | ↓ |

This last exercise based on the G Blues Scale is great for skipping holes.

Ex.16

| 2 | 4 | 3 | 4 | 4 | 5 | 4 | 6 |
|---|---|---|---|---|---|---|---|
| ↓ | ↑ | ↓ | ↓ | ↑ | ↓ | ↓ | ↑ |

# EASY STREET

Up to now we have been playing in the 'straight' position
i.e. the key of C on the C harp. However, from now on we will be playing
in the 'crossed' position i.e. the key of G on our C harp.
This blues solo which is in the key of G will familiarise
you with the 'crossed' position.

Ex.17

# TROUBLE FREE BLUES

Here's a very lively number that will keep you on your toes.
Although it is played quickly you should not have any trouble as it does not
use bends. It is very important at this stage that you can play all the exercises and
solos with ease as the rest of the book includes note bending.

Ex.18

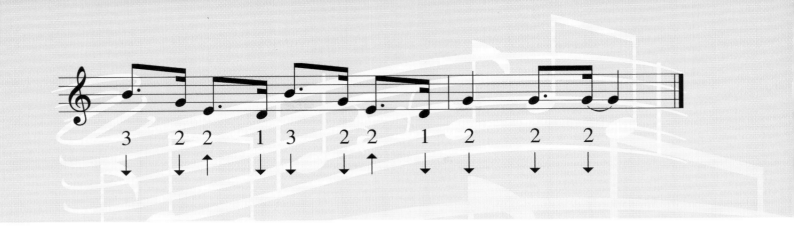

Sonny Boy Williams

# NOTE BENDING

'Note Bending' is a technique which most people find very hard to master,
however, with practice and patience you will soon be able to do it.
It is usually done on the draw notes, from holes 1 to 6.
Lowering the pitch of the note or bending a note involves a certain movement
of your tongue within your mouth.

For example, try whistling a note on an inward breath, then lower it. Notice
how your tongue and jaw change position. This is the same technique we use for
'Note Bending'.

Other phonetic words can be used on the inward breath to achieve bending. For
example, for the normal note say AAAAH! and for the bent note change the
sound to OOOOH!

# D TO D♭ BEND

Now let's start on hole number 4, and practice bending the note.
On our "C" harp, the note is "D" and it will
bend down to "D♭". This is a great note for playing
the blues as it has a real wailing sound.

Remember to get a good "pucker" on the number 4 hole. While you're holding
the pitch, pull your tongue back and down from the opening of your mouth and
apply more pressure from your jaws.

Here is a basic bend exercise.
This time we will add some more notes.

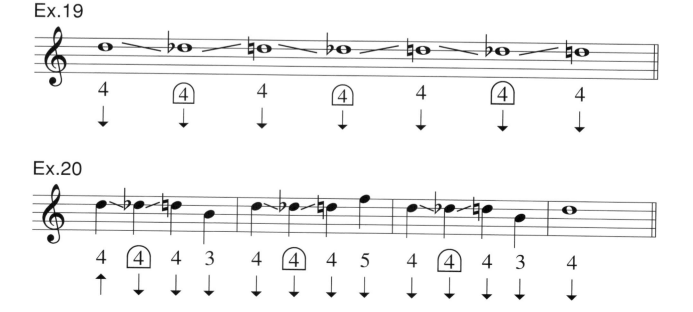

# SUNDRIVE BLUES

This solo features the D to D♭ bend on the 4th hole.
If you can play the previous exercises with ease, then you should have very little
trouble with this solo. At first, you may find yourself hesitating at the notes which
you have to bend, however, with time and practice you will be able to play this
solo smoothly and evenly.

Ex.21

# A TO A♭ BEND

Drawing in your breath on the 6th hole, play the note A.
Then, using the note bending technique bend it down a half tone to A♭.
Here are some exercises for you to practise.

Here is the basic bend exercise.

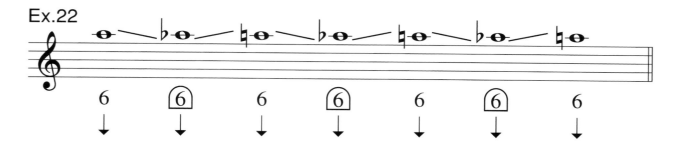

This time we move down to hole 5 after the bend.

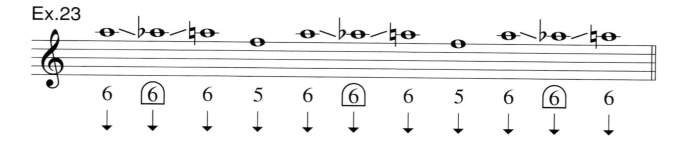

This time we include a blow note on the 7th hole.

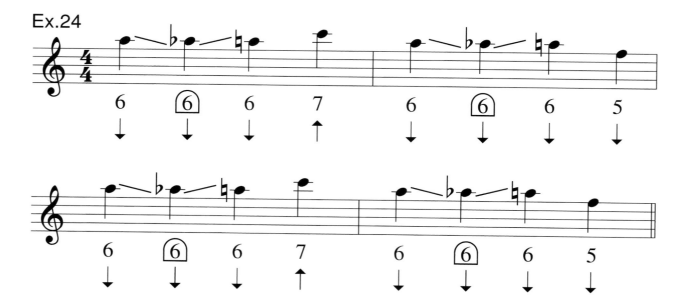

# NOTE BENDING RIFFS
# D TO D♭ and A TO A♭ BEND

Although these riffs sound great on their own they are essentially designed
to help you practice note bending.

This riff features the D to D♭ bend.

**Ex.25**

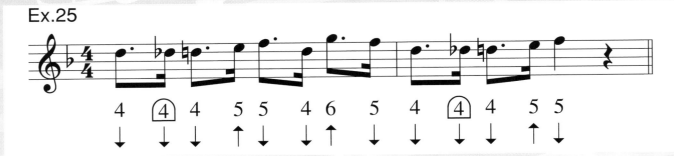

This next riff features the A to A♭ bend.

**Ex.26**

We now have a riff which features the two bends we've dealt with so far.
D to D♭ and A to A♭.

**Ex.27**

**Ex.28**

# BLUE MOOD

This slow blues solo features the A to A♭ bend on the 6th hole.
As we've mentioned before, by the use of note bending you can play in many
keys which, of course, is essential . This solo is in the key of D minor
and again you shouldn't have any trouble with it. However,
you may find the last note a bit long.

# HOT SUMMER BLUES

Up to now the solos have only featured one bend. However, we are
now going to play a solo featuring two bends, D to D♭ and A to A♭.
Just like the last solo it is in a minor key. Most beginners find
playing two or more bends within a solo quite difficult to achieve,
however, with practice, patience and time you won't
have any difficulty with them.

Ex.30

Sonny Boy Williamson

# B TO B♭ BEND

If we draw in our breath on the 3rd hole we will get the
note of B which we are going to bend down to B♭.
The principle is the same as before.

Here is the basic bend exercise.

Ex.31

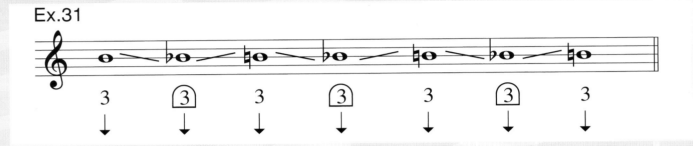

This time we'll add some more notes.

Ex.32

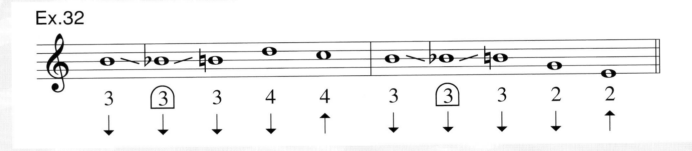

Ex.33

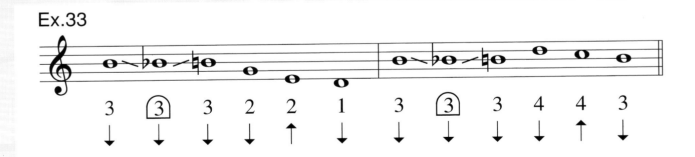

# CLOUDY SKIES

This up tempo solo features the B to B♭ bend on the 3rd hole,
however in bar nine, we have included the D to D♭ bend.
If you have practised all the exercises and solos up to now,
you should be finding the bends easier to play.

Ex.34

# G TO G♭ BEND

Drawing in your breath on the 2nd hole, play the note of G.
Then, using the note bending technique bend it down a half tone to G♭.

Here is the basic bend exercise.

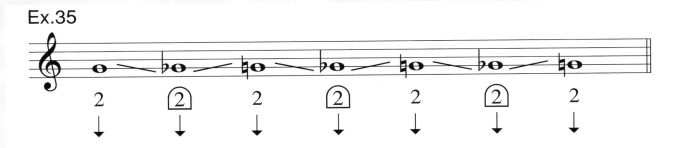

Here we add extra draw notes.

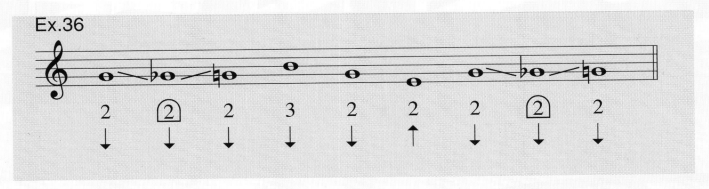

This next exercise is played on holes 1 and 2.

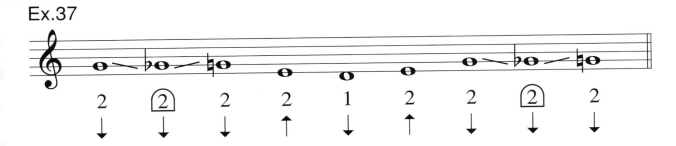

# BLUES RIFFS WITH BENDS

These lively riffs contain all the half tone bends we've dealt with so far.
Make sure you can play these riffs easily before moving on to the next solo.

**Ex.38**

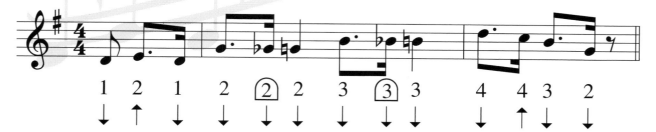

**Ex.39**

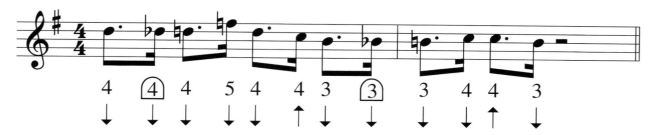

**Ex.40**

**Ex.41**

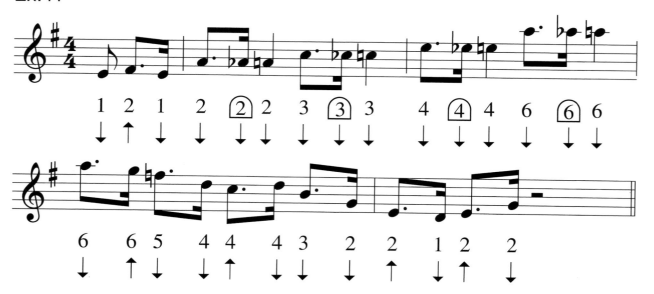

# DOWNTOWN BLUES

This solo features the G to G♭ bend on the 2nd hole along with the D to D♭ bend in bar nine. At this stage it is very important that you can play all the solos that we've learned so far or you will not be able to progress as you should throughout the rest of the book. If you're having difficulties with any of the bends, then I suggest that you go back over all of the previous exercises.

Ex.42

27

# THREE IS A CROWD

This lively tune contains three half tone bends, B to B♭, G to G♭ and D to D♭. It is very important at this stage that you are comfortable with all the previous solos as the next section deals with full tone bends which are a lot more difficult.

Ex.43

Bob Dylan

# FULL TONE BENDS

We will now deal with two full tone bends A and F.
To obtain the A, the note of B on the 3rd hole will have to be bent down two
semitones or one full tone. For the F, bend G on the 2nd hole down a full tone.

Up to now we have only used half, or semitone bends. For the full tone bend
you will need a bit more pressure on the draw note.

Try to create a bigger cavity inside your mouth for the full tone bends.

Say the word YAW! on an inward breath while playing the note.
This will help you achieve a full tone bend.

Here is the basic B to A exercise.

Ex.44

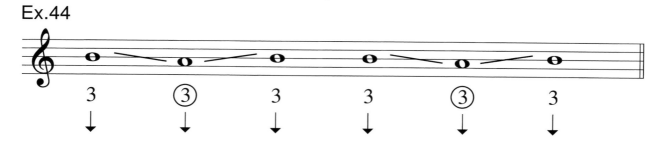

Here is the basic G to F exercise.

Ex.45

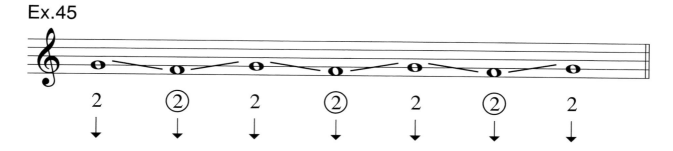

This exercise combines the B to A and G to F full tone bends.

Ex.46

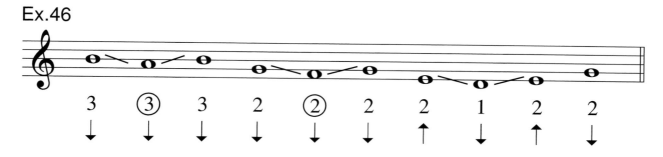

# FULL TONE BEND RIFFS

Not only will these next four riffs help you develop your full tone bends but they are also very enjoyable to play.

**Ex.47**   Riff with B to A full tone bend.

**Ex.48**   Riff with G to F full tone bend.

This next Riff features two full tone bends G down to F and B down to A.

**Ex.49**

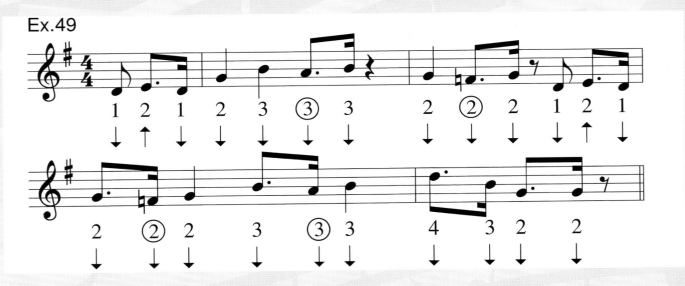

This next exercise features the B to A full tone bend.

**Ex.50**

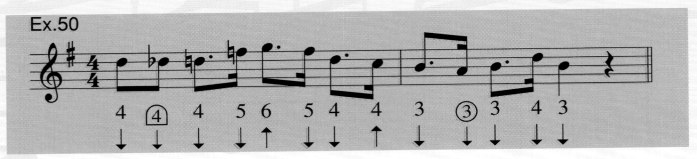

# TWO STEP BLUES

You may find this solo more challenging at first as you will have to play the two
full tone bends we've just dealt with, B to A and G to F.
Don't be discouraged if you can't play them easily within a solo,
most people find this rather difficult to do in the beginning.

Ex.51

# DIRECT BENDING

This is a must and will elevate your playing to a new level
and is a very important technique.
"Direct Bending" is playing a note already bent, for example,
on the 4th hole where we go directly to D♭.
Now the half tone bends are difficult enough
and you will certainly find the full tone "bends" a real challenge,
for example, on the 3rd hole, playing the "bent" note of A.

This is much more difficult than playing a note and then bending
it down which is what we have been doing up to now. With direct
bending the tongue and jaw must already be in the "bent" mode.

There is also a question of pitch. A lot of this technique is in the mind.
You have to imagine what the note sounds like in the "bent" position
and how it feels to bend it the proper amount.

This is not easy so it will take persistence and patience.

Big Mama Thornton

# DIRECT BEND EXERCISES

These exercises will help you with direct bends.
It may feel strange at first, playing a draw note, moving to another and at the same time changing the shape of your mouth, making a deeper cavity to get the note you want.

You should not have too much trouble with this exercise as it only uses the half tone direct bend D♭ up to D.

Ex.52

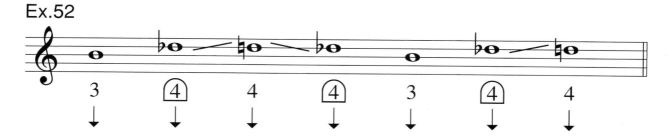

This next exercise is slightly more difficult, as it contains the full tone direct bend from A up to B.

Ex.53

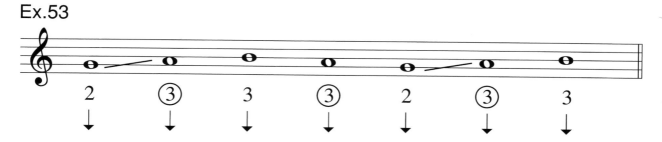

In this exercise we release the bent note F up to G on the same hole.

Ex.54

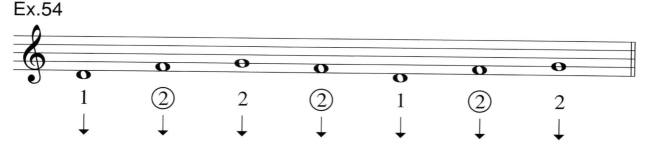

Notice here how you have to change the shape of your mouth from the ordinary inhale note (G), to the deeper cavity for the direct bend to (B♭.)

Ex.55

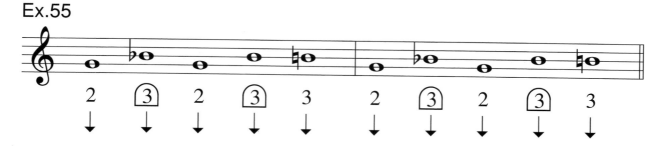

# DIRECT BEND BLUES RIFFS

Here are four great blues riffs for you to try. You may find them rather difficult to play as they feature direct bends, however, with practice and patience you will soon overcome any difficulties you have with them.

**Ex.56**

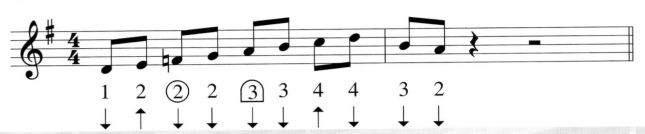

**Ex.57**

**Ex.58**

**Ex.59**

**Ex.60**

# BLUES SCALE IN G

The following scale contains notes that can be played along with just about any blues tune or song in the key of G.

For playing in a "jam session" with other musicians this is an essential scale to learn. You can make up your own riffs as you go along. The scale contains two direct bends B♭ and D♭ which we've just learned.

Ex.61

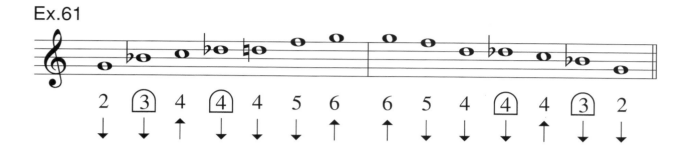

Here is the same scale, however, this time we leave out the direct bend on the 3rd hole (B♭). This version is widely used among blues harp players.

Brownie Mc Ghee + Sonny Terry

Ex.62

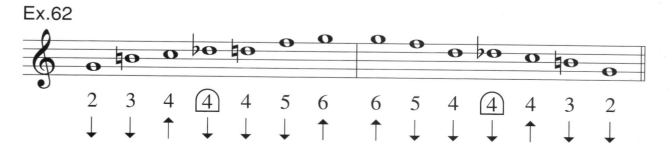

# BLUES SCALE RIFFS

The following riffs are based on the G Blues Scale we've just dealt with. For our first exercise you just play the note B on hole 3. The next three exercises all contain the direct bend from G on hole 2 to B♭ on hole 3.

Ex.63

Ex.64

Ex.65

Ex.66

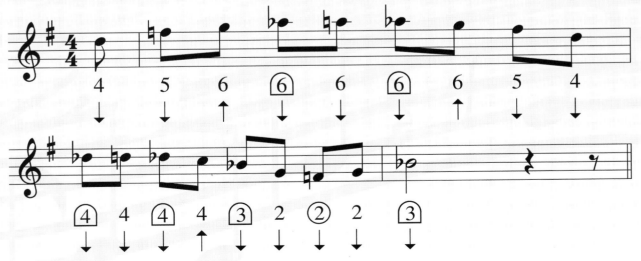

# AFTER MIDNIGHT

This soulful piece makes very good use of the blues scale.
It also includes a new half tone bend on the first hole D to Db.
Watch out for the direct bends on holes 2, 3, 4 and 6.
Also the two semi-tone step down in the fourth bar
which are played on the 2nd hole.

# BLUES RIFFS

Here are some riffs which you will find very useful when playing blues.

**Ex.68**

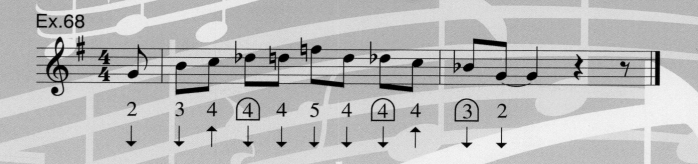

**Ex.69**

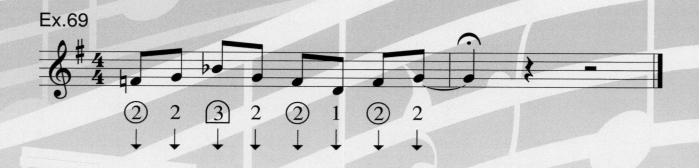

**Ex.70**

**Ex.71**

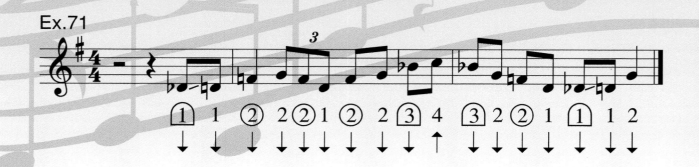

**Ex.72**

**Ex.73**

**Ex.74**

**Ex.75**

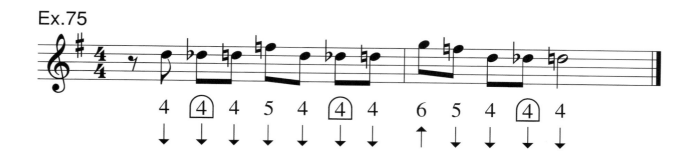

**Ex.76**

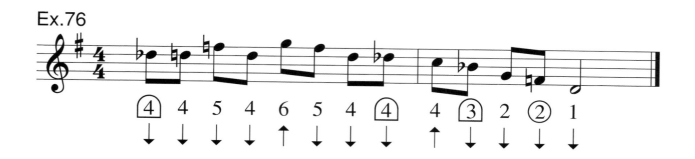

40

# BLOW BENDING

Up to now we have been bending notes on holes from 1 to 6 and this was done using Draw notes. You can also bend notes on the top four holes 7,8,9 and 10, this time by blow bending.

This technique may be achieved by first blowing into one of the top four holes, try hole 8, now bring your tongue forward and slightly tighten the muscles of your jaw. This should cause the note to drop in pitch. You will find the 10th blow note not only difficult to bend, but it is also very hard to keep it in the bent position.

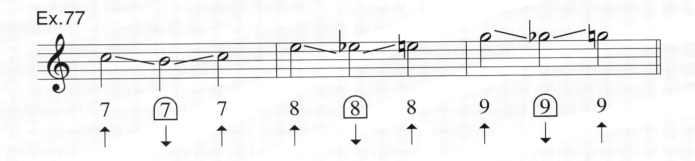

Paul Butterfield

# BLOW BEND RIFFS

You may find some of these 'Blow Bend' riffs more difficult than others. Sometimes the reeds won't respond at all, maybe it's not you, it could be the harp you're using! Some harps are easier to get bends on than others, so why not check out the various brands on the market.

Ex.78

Ex.79

Ex.80

Ex.81

Ex.82

# HIGH TIME BLUES

Now here's a solo which is played in the key of C on our C harp.
It's called 'High Time Blues' and is a style very much associated with
'Chicago and West Coast Harp'.

As this bouncy solo features blow bends on holes 8 and 9 and no other
bends, you will find it very easy to play once you've perfected these.

**Ex.83**

# THE WAH WAH

The "Wah Wah" effect is a great way for producing various sounds and tones.
It is one of the easiest and most popular techniques widely used amongst
blues harp players.

This exciting effect is produced by opening and closing your right hand while
playing the harp using either blow or draw notes. Begin by forming an almost
airtight chamber around the harp, then open and close your
right hand to get the effect.

Ex.84

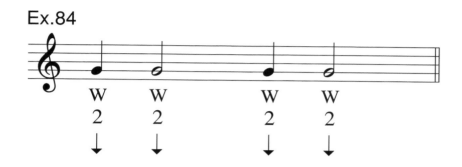

Ex.85

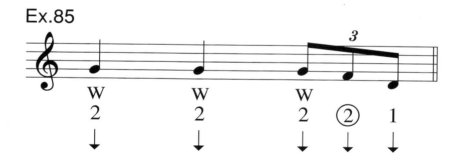

Ex.86

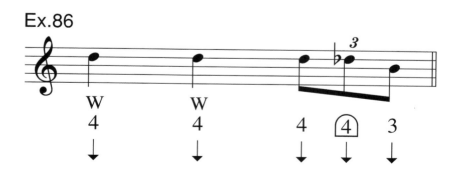

# BLUES RIFFS WITH "WAH WAH"

Here are some great sounding riffs which make full use of the "wah wah". At the beginning of riffs 88 and 89 you have to begin by moving the harp very quickly from side to side to get those fast notes.

Ex.87

Ex.88

Ex.89

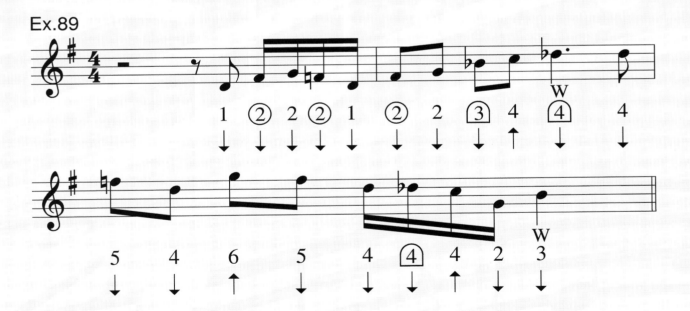

Ex.90

# RAINING DOWN

If you can play all the tunes up to now, you should be well pleased with yourself.
This solo makes great use of wah wah.

Ex.91

# THE HEAD ROLL

Here's a great technique for you to learn and is very popular in blues and country harp music. Technically, these rolls are called trills. The idea is to take two neighbouring notes and move your head very slightly from side to side. This can be done on blow and draw notes. The movement from hole to hole is very slight and should be more like quivering.

In Ex.92 we will start with holes 4 and 5 draw. Begin with hole 4 in your mouth in the normal "Pucker" position, now move to hole 5 and back again to hole 4. Repeat this continually, until you have the roll or trill effect. It is very important that the only notes heard are the two involved. Play these rolls slowly at first then gradually build up speed.
These head rolls can also be played at a slow tempo if you wish.

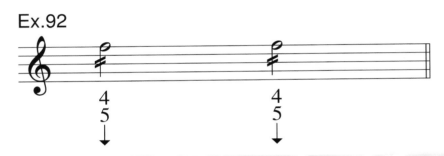

Ex.92

This time we will do a roll on holes 3 and 4.

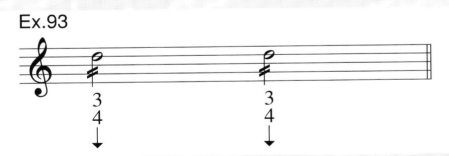

Ex.93

You may find this exercise a little more difficult as you have to play a run of notes before the roll.

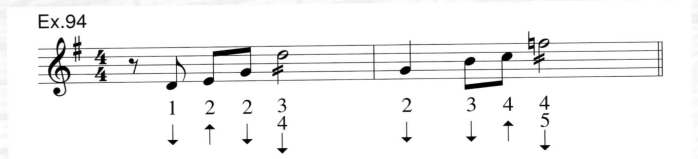

Ex.94

# HEAD ROLL RIFFS

Let's put these head rolls into some riffs now. These five riffs should be played with a really lively and bouncy feel.

**Ex.95**

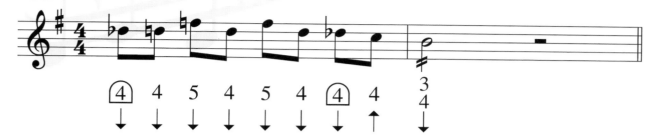

**Ex.96**

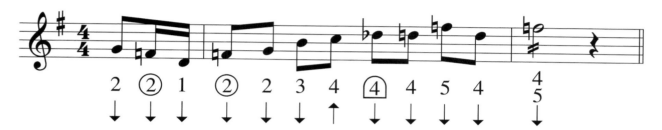

**Ex.97**

**Ex.98**

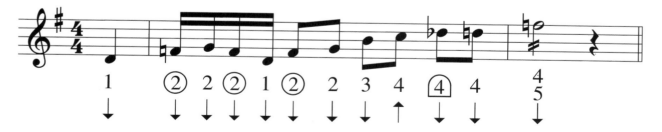

**Ex.99**

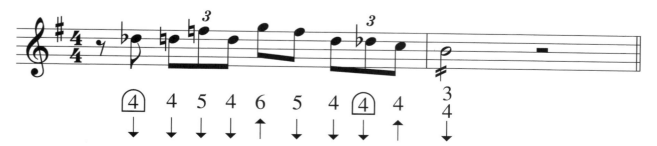

# ROLLING SOUTH

Here's a great little number that makes full use of head rolls. Try this technique on some of the previous solos or indeed any new tunes be it country folk or blues, which I'm sure you must be attempting by now.

Ex.100

# THE TONGUE ROLL

This is another way of doing a roll or trill and again it is played
on two adjacent notes.
Although the effect is the same as the head roll, the tone is quite different.
The tongue roll is easier than the head roll when playing fast tunes.

In this exercise we jump up to the high notes to play a roll.

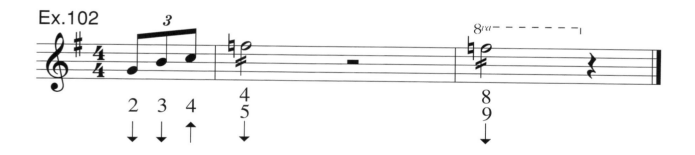

This exercise features a series of tongue rolls.

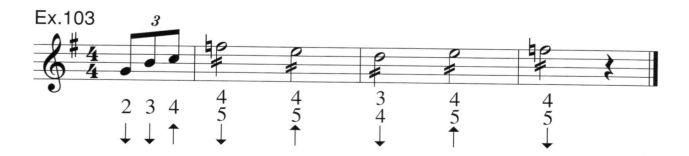

# TONGUE ROLL RIFFS

Make sure to play these riffs without hesitating either going into or coming out of the roll, otherwise the effect will be lost.

### Ex.104

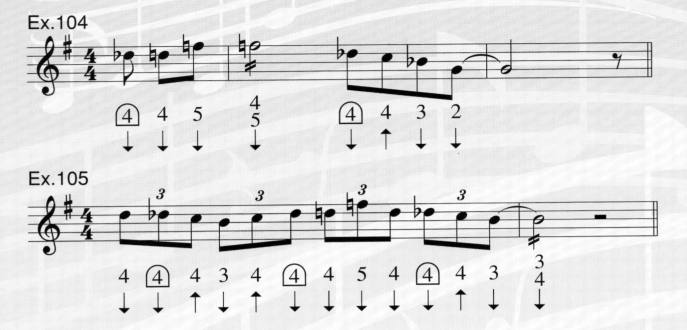

### Ex.105

This one features a series of tongue rolls in the third measure.

### Ex.106

Here is a series of tongue rolls.

### Ex.107

This riff has a very sweet sound, just like a bell.

### Ex.108

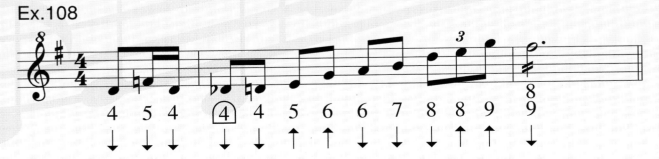

# SOUTHERN JIVE

The tongue roll technique is a major feature of this bright, lively solo.
Make sure the rolls slot nicely into the groove of the tune and that you
are not hesitating at them when they occur.

**Ex.109**

# TONGUE ROLL & WAH WAH

Another great effect while doing a tongue roll is to add the wah wah. However, make sure that you can do the tongue roll with ease before adding the wah wah.

Ex.110

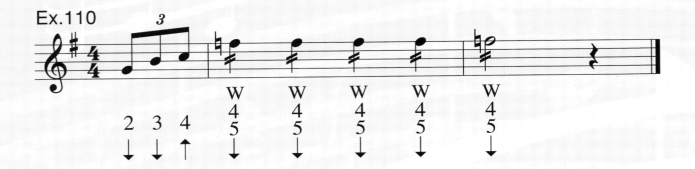

This next exercise features a descending roll including a wah wah on blow and draw notes.

Ex.111

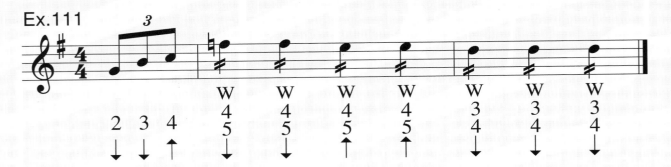

Little Walter

# B L U E S   R I F F S
# WITH TONGUE ROLL AND WAH WAH

The combination of tongue rolls and "wah wah" gives the riffs a very exciting blues sound.

# TROUBLE 'N' BOOZE

The tongue roll and wah wah are played simultaneously in this very soulful blues tune. Try to add some feeling and expression into your playing.

Ex.117

# VIBRATO

An essential part of playing the harp is of course tone control and one of the ways we can achieve this is by the use of vibrato. This will allow you to add feeling and expression to your playing. Try and add some of these vibrato techniques to the tunes you've already learnt.

# SHAKING THE HARP

This vibrato effect can be achieved by quickly shaking the harp up and down slightly while playing. Make sure not to hit the harp on your teeth.

Ex.118

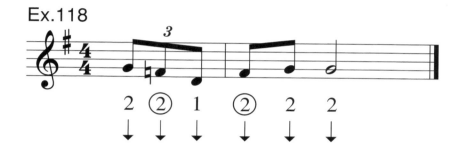

Ex.119

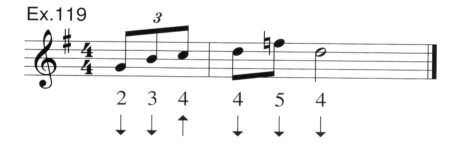

James Cotton

# THROAT VIBRATO

Although this technique is quite difficult, it is well worth mastering as it will help you to develop your own individual tone and sound which is very important.

This vibrato technique is widely used by all the great harp players. Start by drawing in on hole two. Then say the word Eh! repeatedly on the intake of breath like so...

Eh! Eh! Eh! Eh! Eh! Eh! Eh! Eh!....................

This vibrato can also be done in triplet form and can sound great on slow tunes.

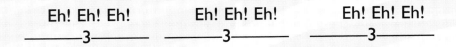

Ex.120

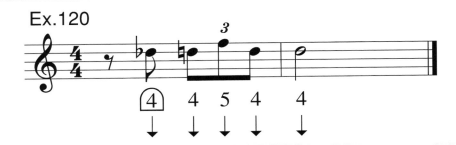

# JAW VIBRATO

I find this vibrato very useful on the bend notes and the top blow bend notes.

First bend a note, for example, the full tone bend from B to A on hole 3. When you reach the note of A, try saying the words

Yuh! Yuh! Yuh! .....................

while keeping the notes in the bent position.
Try these two vibratos on the solos we've dealt with earlier on.

Now try this exercise.

Ex.121

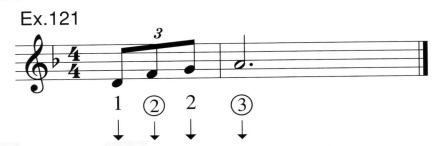

# BLUES RIFFS USING TONE CONTROL

By using the various vibrato techniques which we've discussed you can make your harp weep or wail on these very soulful blues riffs.

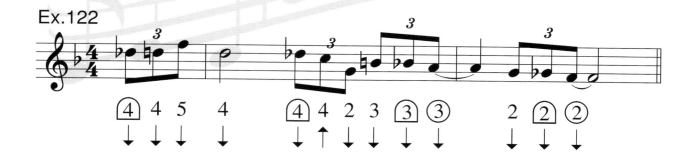

Ex.122

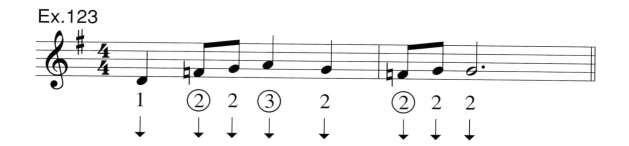

Ex.123

Ex.124

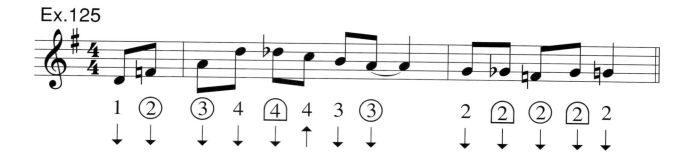

Ex.125

# NOTE SPLITTING

This is a term used to describe the blocking of one or more holes with the tongue. For example, to do an octave split we place our mouth over holes 1 to 4 then press our tongue against holes 2 and 3 so that the notes can only be produced from holes 1 and 4. Now if we blow on these two holes we will be playing two C notes which are an octave apart.

You may find this exercise a little more difficult as you have to move up and down the harp while tongue blocking.

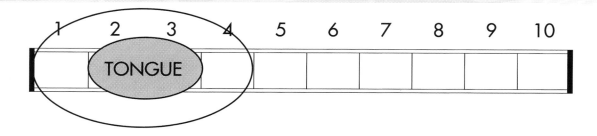

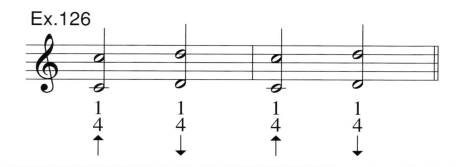

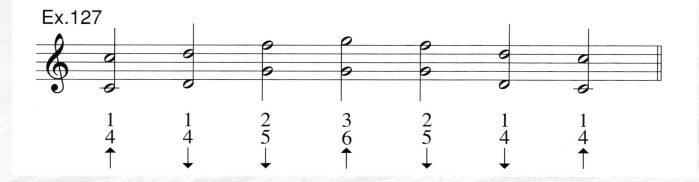

# NOTE SPLITTING RIFFS

This next set of riffs should be played with a very bouncy feel. Make sure you can play them easily before attempting our final solo.

# LAKE SHORE DRIVE
## (INTRO SOLO)

The main feature of this shuffle type number is note splitting. You may find
alternating between single and split notes quite challenging,
however, as the old adage goes... 'Practice makes Perfect'.